PLUTONIAN ODE

Poems 1977-1980

ALLEN GINSBERG

"La science, la nouvelle noblesse! Le progrès. Le monde marche!
Pourquoi ne tournerait-il pas?"
— *Rimbaud*

The Pocket Poets Series: Number Forty

CITY LIGHTS BOOKS
San Francisco

© 1982 by Allen Ginsberg

First printing: January 1982

Music by Allen Ginsberg, notation by Steven Taylor, script by Jon Sholle.

Library of Congress Cataloging in Publication Data:

Ginsberg, Allen, 1926-
   Plutonian Ode.

    (Pocket poets series; no. 40)
   I: Title.
PS3513.174P63   811'.54   81-7657
ISBN 0-87286-126-0   AACR2
ISBN 0-87286-125-2 (pbk.)

CITY LIGHTS BOOKS are edited by Lawrence Ferlinghetti & Nancy J. Peters, and published at the City Lights Bookstore, 261 Columbus Avenue, San Francisco, California 94133.

dedicated
for friendship
all these years
to
Lucien Carr

This poetry was first printed in the following papers, books, magazines, mimeos, calendars, and broadsides:

Aquarian; Alternative Press Broadside; American Poetry Review; *A Year of Disobedience;* Beatitude; Bernerzeitung; Birthstone; Bombay Gin; Boulder Monthly; Boulder Street Poets; Carl Kay; Clean Energy Verse; Cody's Bookshop Calendar; Coevolution Quarterly; Dirty; El Dorado H.S.; Expressen; Firefly Press; Gay Sunshine; Greenpeace; Harvard Crimson; Harvard Mgazine; High Times; Ins & Outs; Intrepid; L.A. Times; Mag City; Mutantia; Nuke Chronicles; Old Pond Songs; Passaic Review; Pearl; Piazza; Poetry London/Apple; Poetry on the Tracks; Poetry Toronto; Poets-and-Writers; Quixote; Read Street; River Run; River Styx; Rocky Flats Truth Force; Rocky Ledge; Rolling Stone; Saturday Morning; Spradie im Technisehen Zeitalter; Takeover; The Grapevine; Throat; Utigeverij 261; Vancouver Vajradhatu; Vajradhatu Sun; Village Voice; Vigencia; Walker Art Center Broadside; West Hills Review; W.I.N. Magazine; The Nation; Zero.

Part of this book was written and all assembled during period of National Endowment for the Arts Fellowship and N.Y. State Creative Artists Programs Service, Inc. Grant, 1980 to the author.

Final typescripts were assembled at the home office, Lower East Side, New York City, N.Y. by Bob Rosenthal and Ron Lieber, and at Boulder Naropa Institute's Jack Kerouac School of Disembodied Poetics by many apprentice students 1981 including Sam Kashner, Helen Luster, Denise King & Gary Allen.

CONTENTS

PLUTONIAN ODE

Allen Ginsberg, Peter Orlovsky and friends of Rocky Flats Truth Force, meditating on R.R. Tracks outside Rockwell Corporation Nuclear Facility's Plutonium bomb trigger factory, Colorado, halting trainload of waste fissile materials on the day Plutonian Ode was completed, July 14, 1978. photo by Joe Daniel

PLUTONIAN ODE

I

1   What new element before us unborn in nature? Is there
a new thing under the Sun?

At last inquisitive Whitman a modern epic, detonative,
Scientific theme

First penned unmindful by Doctor Seaborg with poison-
ous hand, named for Death's planet through the
sea beyond Uranus

whose chthonic ore fathers this magma-teared Lord of
Hades, Sire of avenging Furies, billionaire Hell-
King worshipped once

5   with black sheep throats cut, priest's face averted from
underground mysteries in a single temple at Eleusis,

Spring-green Persephone nuptialed to his inevitable
Shade, Demeter mother of asphodel weeping dew,

her daughter stored in salty caverns under white snow,
black hail, grey winter rain or Polar ice, immemor-
able seasons before

Fish flew in Heaven, before a Ram died by the starry
bush, before the Bull stamped sky and earth

or Twins inscribed their memories in clay or Crab'd
flood

10   washed memory from the skull, or Lion sniffed the
lilac breeze in Eden—

Before the Great Year began turning its twelve signs,
 ere constellations wheeled for twenty-four thousand
 sunny years
slowly round their axis in Sagittarius, one hundred
 sixty-seven thousand times returning to this night

Radioactive Nemesis were you there at the beginning
 black Dumb tongueless unsmelling blast of Disil-
 lusion?
I manifest your Baptismal Word after four billion years
15 I guess your birthday in Earthling Night, I salute your
 dreadful presence lasting majestic as the Gods,
Sabaot, Jehova, Astapheus, Adonaeus, Elohim, Iao,
 Ialdabaoth, Aeon from Aeon born ignorant in an
 Abyss of Light,
Sophia's reflections glittering thoughtful galaxies, whirl-
 pools of starspume silver-thin as hairs of Einstein!
Father Whitman I celebrate a matter that renders Self
 oblivion!
Grand Subject that annihilates inky hands & pages'
 prayers, old orators' inspired Immortalities,
20 I begin your chant, openmouthed exhaling into spacious
 sky over silent mills at Hanford, Savannah River,
 Rocky Flats, Pantex, Burlington, Albuquerque
I yell thru Washington, South Carolina, Colorado,
 Texas, Iowa, New Mexico,
where nuclear reactors create a new Thing under the
 Sun, where Rockwell war-plants fabricate this death
 stuff trigger in nitrogen baths,

Hanger-Silas Mason assembles the terrified weapon
secret by ten thousands, & where Manzano Moun-
tain boasts to store
its dreadful decay through two hundred forty millenia
while our Galaxy spirals around its nebulous core.
25 I enter your secret places with my mind, I speak with
your presence, I roar your Lion Roar with mortal
mouth.
One microgram inspired to one lung, ten pounds of
heavy metal dust adrift slow motion over grey
Alps
the breadth of the planet, how long before your radiance
speeds blight and death to sentient beings?
Enter my body or not I carol my spirit inside you,
Unapproachable Weight,
O heavy heavy Element awakened I vocalize your con-
sciousness to six worlds
30 I chant your absolute Vanity. Yeah monster of Anger
birthed in fear O most
Ignorant matter ever created unnatural to Earth! Delusion
of metal empires!
Destroyer of lying Scientists! Devourer of covetous
Generals, Incinerator of Armies & Melter of Wars!
Judgement of judgements, Divine Wind over vengeful
nations, Molester of Presidents, Death-Scandal of
Capital politics! Ah civilizations stupidly indus-
trious!

Canker-Hex on multitudes learned or illiterate! Manufactured Spectre of human reason! O solidified imago of practitioners in Black Arts

35 I dare your Reality, I challenge your very being! I publish your cause and effect!

I turn the Wheel of Mind on your three hundred tons! Your name enters mankind's ear! I embody your ultimate powers!

My oratory advances on your vaunted Mystery! This breath dispels your braggart fears! I sing your form at last

behind your concrete & iron walls inside your fortress of rubber & translucent silicon shields in filtered cabinets and baths of lathe oil,

My voice resounds through robot glove boxes & ingot cans and echoes in electric vaults inert of atmosphere,

40 I enter with spirit out loud into your fuel rod drums underground on soundless thrones and beds of lead

O density! This weightless anthem trumpets transcendent through hidden chambers and breaks through iron doors into the Infernal Room!

Over your dreadful vibration this measured harmony floats audible, these jubilant tones are honey and milk and wine-sweet water

Poured on the stone block floor, these syllables are barley groats I scatter on the Reactor's core,

I call your name with hollow vowels, I psalm your Fate
    close by, my breath near deathless ever at your
    side
45   to Spell your destiny, I set this verse prophetic on your
    mausoleum walls to seal you up Eternally with
    Diamond Truth! O doomed Plutonium.

II

The Bard surveys Plutonian history from midnight
    lit with Mercury Vapor streetlamps till in dawn's
    early light
he contemplates a tranquil politic spaced out between
    Nations' thought-forms proliferating bureaucratic
& horrific arm'd, Satanic industries projected sudden
    with Five Hundred Billion Dollar Strength
around the world same time this text is set in Boulder,
    Colorado before front range of Rocky Mountains
50   twelve miles north of Rocky Flats Nuclear Facility in
    United States on North America, Western Hemi-
    sphere
of planet Earth six months and fourteen days around
    our Solar System in a Spiral Galaxy
the local year after Dominion of the last God nineteen
    hundred seventy eight

Completed as yellow hazed dawn clouds brighten East,
Denver city white below
Blue sky transparent rising empty deep & spacious to a
morning star high over the balcony
55   above some autos sat with wheels to curb downhill
from Flatiron's jagged pine ridge,
sunlit mountain meadows sloped to rust-red sandstone
cliffs above brick townhouse roofs
as sparrows waked whistling through Marine Street's
summer green leafed trees.

III

This ode to you O Poets and Orators to come, you
father Whitman as I join your side, you Congress
and American people,
you present meditators, spiritual friends & teachers,
you O Master of the Diamond Arts,
60   Take this wheel of syllables in hand, these vowels and
consonants to breath's end
take this inhalation of black poison to your heart, breathe
out this blessing from your breast on our creation
forests cities oceans deserts rocky flats and mountains
in the Ten Directions pacify with this exhalation,
enrich this Plutonian Ode to explode its empty thunder
through earthen thought-worlds

Magnetize this howl with heartless compassion, destroy
this mountain of Plutonium with ordinary mind
and body speech,
65   thus empower this Mind-guard spirit gone out, gone
out, gone beyond, gone beyond me, Wake space,
so Ah!

Verse

2: *Walt Whitman*

3: *sea: Pluto, past planets Uranus and Neptune. Dr. Glen Seaborg, "Discoverer of Plutonium."*

4: *Pluto was father to Eumenides, the Furies who return to avenge mindless damage done in passion, aggression, ignorance, etc. Pluto was also Lord of Wealth.*

6: *Demeter: Pluto's mother-in-law, the Earth fertility goddess whose daughter Persephone was stolen for marriage by underworld lord Pluto & kept his caverns a half year at a time, released to her mother each spring. Demeter gave wheat to man at Eleusis, site of her temple, one place in ancient world where Pluto was also worshipped with ceremonies indicated above.*

7. *W. C. Williams wrote of Asphodel "that greeny flower" as the blossom of Hades.*

8: *Fish, Ram, Bull, Twins, Crab, Lion: Ages of Pisces, Aries, Taurus, Gemini, Cancer, Leo. 2000 years each age.*

11: *Platonic, or Babylonian or Sidereal "Great Year"=24,000 years=half life of Plutonium radioactivity. This fact, pointed out to me by Gregory Corso, inspired this Poem.*

12: *The 24,000 year span of the Great Year=167,000 cycles=4 Billion Years, supposed Age of Earth.*

13: *Ref.: Six senses including mind.*

16: *Jehova to Ialdabaoth: Archons of successive Aeons born of Sophia's thought, according to Ophitic & Barbelo-Gnostic myths.*

20-23: *Plutonium Factories, whose location by state and whose function in Bomb-making are here described.*

24: *240,000 years the supposed time till Plutonium becomes physically inert.*

26-27: *Ten pounds of Plutonium scatterd throughout the earth is calculated sufficient to kill 4 Billion people.*

29: *Six worlds of Gods, Warrior Demons, Humans, Hungry Ghosts, Animals, & Hell Beings held together in the delusion of time by pride, anger & ignorance: a Buddhist concept.*

33: *Divine Wind=kamikaze, typhoon, wind of Gods.*

36: *300 tons of Plutonium, estimate circa 1978 of the amount produced for American bombs.*

37: *"I sing your form" etc. "The Reactor hath hid himself thro envy. I behold him. But you cannot behold him till he be revealed in his System." Blake, Jerusalem, Chapter II Plate 43 1. 9-10.*

43: *Traditional libation to Hades poured at Temple of Eleusis, and by Odysseus at the Necromanteion at Acheron.*

45: *Diamond: ref. to Buddhist doctrine of Sunyata, i.e. existence as simultaneously void and solid, empty and real, all-penetrating egoless (empty void) nature symbolized by adamantine Vajra or Diamond Sceptre.*

48: *Estimated World Military Budget, 116 Billion U.S. share, Oct. 1978.*

61-63: *Four characteristics of Buddha-nature activity: to pacify, enrich, magnetize & destroy.*

65: *Americanese approximation & paraphrase of Sanscrit Prajnaparamita (Highest Perfect Wisdom) Mantra: Gate Gate Paragate Parasamgate Bodhi Svaha.*

POEMS: 1977-1980

STOOL PIGEON BLUES

I was born in Wyoming, Cody is my home town
Got myself busted, the sheriff brought me down
The Feds hit my nose, I felt like a dirty Clown

I turned in my sister, just like they asked me to
I turned in my brother, I had to, wouldn't you?
If they beat me again, I guess I'd turn you in too

Please don't blame me, they had me for twenty years
An ounce of weed, they planted it in my ears
They found one seed, and watered it with my tears

I got A's in highschool, smartest boy in class
Got laid at eleven, the sweetest piece of ass
They found us in bed smoking a stick of grass

Girl broke down crying, the Narcs liked her looks in the nude
Asked us for blowjobs, I told them that was too crude
Took us to jail & accused us of being lewd

Ten years for resisting arrest, ten years for a little joint
Ten years kid, beginning to get the point?
Feds want a big bust, let's hear you sing oink oink!

Who do you know in highschool, how many's dealing lids?
Who do you smoke with? We want the names of kids.
They'll bust all our parents, unless Good God forbids!

I'm just a poor stoolie, got busted in Wyoming
From Cody, to Casper, to Riverton I will sing!
From Gilette to Powell a pigeon I'm on the wing.

Governor Governor Get me out of this fix!
President President decriminalize the sticks,
Out here in Wyoming, Sheriffs play dirty tricks.

April 16, 1977

PUNK ROCK YOUR MY BIG CRYBABY

I'll tell my deaf mother on you! Fall on the floor
and eat your grandmother's diapers! Drums,
Whatta lotta Noise you want a Revolution?
Wanna Apocalypse? Blow up in Dynamite Sound?
I can't get excited, Louder! Viciouser!
Fuck me in the ass! Suck me! Come in my ears!
I want those pink Abdominal bellybuttons!
Promise you'll murder me in the gutter with Orgasms!
I'll buy a ticket to your nightclub, I wanna get busted!
50 years old I wanna Go! with whips & chains & leather!
Spank me! Kiss me in the eye! Suck me all over
from Mabuhay Gardens to CBGB's coast to coast
Skull to toe Gimme yr electric guitar naked,
Punk President, eat up the FBI w/ yr big mouth.

Mabuhay Gardens, May 1977

WHAT'S DEAD?

Clouds' silent shadows passing across the Sun above Teton's
    mountaintop I saw on LSD
Movies dead shadows
ocean 40% dead said expert J. Cousteau A.D. 1968
Shakespeare the magician, Rimbaud visionary dead
silent vamp Alla Nazimova's corpse-lip black dust
Walt Disney of Mickey Mouse, Buck Rogers in the Twenty-
    fifth Century, Hollywood lost in shade
Tragedean Sophocles passed this shore with Charon thru
    Styx
Ex-Emperor Napoleon obituaried in 1822
Queen Liliuokalani giv'n to her reward
Chief Joseph buried on a brown hill in Washington State
General Douglas MacArthur urged atombombs to blow up
    China
Eisenhower & Xerxes led armies to the grave
The Skeleton Man in 1930 Barnum & Bailey Circus' Freak-
    show bony in's coffin
The mother Cat I played with in the basement Paterson
    New Jersey when I was ten
with the Lindbergh baby kidnapped found in a swamp of
    laundry
My father's grave writ "Answer a riddle with a stone" wet
    with rain in Newark
Jesus Christ & Mary for all their Assumption, dust in this
    world

Buddha relieved his body, empty vehicle parked noiseless
Allah the Word in a book, or muezzin cry on a Tower
Not even Moses reached Promised Land, went down to Sheol.
Tickertape for heroes, clods of dirt for forgotten grandpas—
Television ghosts still haunt living room & bed chamber
Crooner Bing Crosby, Elvis Presley rock'n'roll Star, Groucho
      Marx a mustached joker, Einstein invented the uni-
      verse, Naomi Ginsberg Communist Muse, Isadora
      Duncan dancing in diaphanous scarves
Jack Kerouac noble Poet, Jimmy Dean mystic actor, Boris
      Karloff the old Frankenstein,
Celebrities & Nonentities set apart, absent from their paths
      shadows left behind, breathing no more—
These were the musings of Buddhist student Allen Ginsberg.

October 16, 1977

GRIM SKELETON

Grim skeleton come back & put me out of Action
looking thru the rainy window at the Church wall
yellow vapor lamped, 9pm Cars hissing in street water
—woken dizzy from nicotine sleep—papers piled on
    my desk
myself lost in manila files of yellow faded newspaper
    Clippings
at last after twenty five years tapes wound thru my brain
Library of my own deeds of music tongue & oratoric yell—
Is it my heart, a cold & phlegm in my skull or radiator
Comfort cowardice that I slumber awake wrapped in
    Mexican
Blanket, wallet & keys on the white chair by my head.
Is it the guru of music or guru of meditation whose
    harsh force
I bear, makes my eyelid heavy mid afternoons, is't Death
stealing in my breast makes me nauseous mornings, work
    undone
on a typewriter set like a green skull by the window
When I wake unwilling to rise & take the narcotic *Times*
above a soft Boiled egg and toasted English muffin daily
    noon?
Beauty, Truth, Revolution, what skeleton in my closet
makes me listen dumb my own skull thoughts lethargic

Gossip of Poets silenced by drunken Mussolinis every
    Country on Earth?

My own yatter of meditation, while I work and scream
    in frenzy

at my wooden desk held up by iron filedrawers stuffed
    w/press paper

& prophetic fake manuscripts, ears itching & scabbed
    w/anger

at ghost Rockefeller Brothers pay-off of CIA, am I myself
    the CIA

bought with acid meat & alcohol in Washington, silenced
    in meditation

on my own duplicity, stuck in anger at puerto rican
    wounded

beerdrunk fathers walking East 12th street and their
    thieving kids

violent screaming under my window 4 AM? Some Fantasy
    of Fame

I dreamt in adolescence Came true last week over
    Television,

Now homunculus I made's out there in American streets

talking with my voice, accounted ledgered opinionated

Interviewed & Codified in Poems, books & manuscripts,
    whole library

shelves stacked with ambitious egohood's thousand pages
    imaged

forth smart selft over half a lifetime! Who'm I now,
    Frankenstein

hypocrite of good Cheer whose sick-stomached
     Discretion's grown
fifty years overweight—while others I hate practice saint-
     hood in Himalayas
or run the petrochemical atomic lamplit machines,
     by whose power
I slumber cook my meat & write these verses captive
     of N.Y.C.
What's my sickness, flu virus or selfhood infected
     swollen sore
confronting the loath'd work of poetic flattery: Gurus,
     Rock stars
Penthoused millionaires, White House alrightnicks
     crowding my brain
with orders & formulae, insults & smalltalk, threats
     & dollars
Whose sucker am I, the media run by rich whitemen like
     myself, jew
intellectuals afraid of poverty bust screaming beaten
     uncontrolled behind bars
or the black hole of narcotics Cops & brutal Mafiosi, thick
     men in dark hats,
hells angels in blue military garb or wall street cashmere
     drag
hiding iron muscles of money, so the street is full of
     potholes, I'm afraid
to go out at night around the block to look at the moon in
     the Lower East Side

where stricken junkes break their necks in damp
    hallways of
abandoned buildings gutted & blackwindowed from old
    fires. I'm afraid
to write my thoughts down lest I libel Nelson Rockefeller,
    Fidel
Castro, Chögyam Trungpa, Louis Ginsberg & Naomi, Kerouac
    or Peter O.
yea Henry Kissinger & Richard Helms, faded ghosts of
    Power and Poesy
that people my brain with paranoia, my best friend
    shall be Nameless.
Whose public speech is this I write? What stupid vast
    Complaint!
For what impotent professor's ears, which Newsman's
    brainwave? What jazz king's devil blues?
Is this Immortal history to tell tales of 20th Century to
    striplings
naked centuries hence? To get laid by some brutal
    queen who'll
beat my hairy buttocks punishment in a College Dorm?
    To show my ass
to god? To grovel in magic tinsel & glitter on stinking
    powdered pillows?
Agh! Who'll I read this to like a fool! Who'll applaud
    these lies

Dec. 16, 1977

LACK LOVE

Love wears down to bare truth
My heart hurt me much in youth
Now I hear my real heart beat
Strong and hollow thump of meat

I felt my heart wrong as an ache
Sore in dreams and raw awake
I'd kiss each new love on the breast
Trembling hug him breast to breast

Kiss his belly, kiss his eye
Kiss his ruddy boyish thigh
Kiss his feet kiss his pink cheek
Kiss behind him naked meek

Now I lie alone, and a youth
Stalks my house, he won't in truth
Come to bed with me, instead
Loves the thoughts inside my head

He knows how much I think of him
Holds my heart his painful whim
Looks thru me with mocking eyes
Steals my feelings, drinks & lies

Till I see Love's empty Truth
Think back on heart broken youth
Hear my heart beat red in bed
Thick and living, love rejected.

3 am Feb 8, 1978

FATHER GURU

Father Guru   unforlorn
Heart beat Guru whom I scorn
Empty Guru Never Born
Sitting Guru every morn
Friendly Guru chewing corn
Angry Guru Faking Porn
Guru Guru Freely torn
Garment Guru neatly worn
Guru Head short hair shorn
Absent Guru   Eyes I mourn
Guru of Duncan Guru of Dorn
Ginsberg Guru like a thorn
Goofy Guru Lion Horn
Lonely Guru Unicorn
O Guru whose slave I'm sworn
Save me Guru Om Ah Hūṃ

February 14, 1978

MANHATTAN MAY DAY MIDNIGHT

I walked out on the lamp shadowed concrete at midnight
    May Day passing a dark'd barfront,
police found corpses under the floor last year, call-girls &
    Cadillacs lurked there on First Avenue
around the block from my apartment, I'd come downstairs
    for tonight's newspapers —
refrigerator repair shop's window grate padlocked, fluores-
    cent blue
light on a pile of newspapers, pages shifting in the chill
    Spring
wind 'round battered cans & plastic refuse bags leaned to-
    gether at the pavement edge —
Wind wind and old news sailed thru the air, old *Times* whirled
    above the garbage.
At the Corner of 11th under dim Street-light in a hole in the
    ground
a man wrapped in work-Cloth and wool Cap pulled down his
    bullet skull
stood & bent with a rod & flashlight turning round in his pit
    halfway sunk in earth
Peering down at his feet, up to his chest in the asphalt by a
    granite Curb
where his work mate poked a flexible tube in a tiny hole, a
    youth in gloves
who answered my question "Smell of gas — Someone must've
    reported in" —

Yes the body stink of City bowels, rotting tubes six feet under
Could explode any minute sparked by Con Ed's breathing
     Puttering truck
I noticed parked, as I passed by hurriedly Thinking Ancient
     Rome, Ur
Were they like this, the same shadowy surveyors & passers-by
scribing records of decaying pipes & Garbage piles on Marble,
     Cuneiform,
ordinary midnight citizen out on the street looking for Empire
     News,
rumor, gossip, workmen police in uniform, walking silent
     sunk in thought
under windows of sleepers coupled with Monster squids &
     Other-Planet eyeballs in their sheets
in the same night six thousand years old where Cities rise &
     fall & turn to dream?

6 am 1978

Adapted from
NERUDA'S "QUE DISPIERTE
EL LENADOR"

V

Let the Railsplitter Awake!
Let Lincoln come with his axe
and with his wooden plate
to eat with the farmworkers.
May his craggy head,
his eyes we see in constellations,
in the wrinkles of the live oak,
come back to look at the world
rising up over the foliage
higher than Sequoias.
Let him go shop in pharmacies,
let him take the bus to Tampa
let him nibble a yellow apple,
let him go to the movies, and
talk to everybody there.

Let the Railsplitter awake!

Let Abraham come back, let his old yeast
rise in green and gold earth of Illinois,
and lift the axe in his city
against the new slavemakers

against their slave whips
against the venom of the print houses
against all the bloodsoaked
merchandise they want to sell.
Let the young white boy and young black
march singing and smiling
against walls of gold,
against manufacturers of hatred,
against the seller of his own blood,
singing, smiling and winning at last.

Let the Railsplitter awake!

VI

Peace for all twilights to come,
peace for the bridge, peace for the wine,
peace for the letters that look for me
and pump in my blood tangled
with earth and love's old chant,
peace for the city in the morning
when bread wakes up,
peace for Mississippi, the river of roots,
peace for my brother's shirt,
peace in the book like an airmail stamp,
peace for the great Kolkhoz of Kiev,
peace for the ashes of these dead
and those other dead, peace for the black
iron of Booklyn, peace for the lettercarrier

going from house to house like the day,
peace for the choreographer shrieking
thru a funnel of honeysuckle vines,
peace to my right hand
that only wants to write Rosario,
peace for the Bolivian, secret as a lump of tin,
peace for you to get married, peace
for all the sawmills of Bio Bio,
peace to Revolutionary Spain's torn heart
peace to the little museum of Wyoming
in which the sweetest thing
was a pillowcase embroidered with a heart,
peace to the baker and his loves,
and peace to all the flour: peace
for all the wheat still to be born,
peace for all the love that wants to flower,
peace for all those who live: peace
to all the lands and waters.

And here I say farewell, I return
to my house, in my dreams
I go back to Patagonia where
the wind beats at barns
and the Ocean spits ice.
I'm nothing more than a poet:
I want love for you all,
I go wander the world I love:
in my country they jail the miners
and soldiers give orders to judges.

But down to its very roots
I love my little cold country.
If I had to die a thousand times
that's where I'd want to die:
if I had to be born a thousand times
that's where I'd want to be born,
near the Araucarian wilds'
sea-whirled south winds,
bells just brought from the bellmaker.
Don't let anybody think about me.
Let's think about the whole world,
banging on the table with love.
I don't want blood to come back
and soak the bread, the beans
the music: I want the miner
to come with me, the little girl,
the lawyer, the sailor, the dollmaker,
let's all go to the movies and come
out and drink the reddest wine.

I didn't come here to solve anything.

I came here to sing
And for you to sing with me.

Adapted Summer 1978—Spring 1981 by Sidney Goldfarb and Allen Ginsberg from Waldeen's Tr. of Let The Railsplitter Awake And Other Poems, *by Pablo Neruda. New York: Masses and Mainstream, 1950.*

NAGASAKI DAYS

I — A Pleasant Afternoon

for Michael Brownstein & Dick Gallup

One day 3 poets & 60 ears sat under a green-striped Chau-
    tauqua tent in Aurora
listening to Black spirituals, tapping their feet, appreciating
    words singing by in mountain winds
on a pleasant sunny day of rest—the wild wind blew thru
    blue Heavens
filled with fluffy clouds stretched from Central City to Rocky
    Flats, Plutonium sizzled in its secret bed,
hot dogs sizzled in the Lion's Club lunchwagon microwave
    mouth, orangeade bubbled over in waxen cups
Traffic moved along Colefax, meditators silent in the Diamond
    Castle shrine-room at Boulder followed the breath going
    out of their nostrils,
Nobody could remember anything, spirits flew out of mouths
    & noses, out of the sky, across Colorado plains & the
    tent flapped happily open spacious & didn't fall down.

June 18, 1978

II — Peace Protest

Cumulus clouds float across blue sky
      over the white-walled Rockwell Corporation factory
                — am I going to stop that?

*

Rocky Mountains rising behind us
      Denver shining in morning light
— Led away from the crowd by police and photographers

*

Middleaged Ginsberg & Ellsberg taken down the road
      to the greyhaired Sheriff's van —
But what about Einstein? What about Einstein? Hey, Einstein
                Come back!

III — Golden Courthouse

Waiting for the Judge, breathing silent
      Prisoners, witnesses, Police —
the stenographer yawns into her palms.

August 9, 1978

IV—Everybody's Fantasy

I walked outside & the bomb'd
     dropped lots of plutonium
     all over the Lower East Side
There weren't any buildings left just
     iron skeletons
groceries burned, potholes open to
     stinking sewer waters

There were people starving and crawling
     across the desert
the Martian UFOs with blue
     Light destroyer rays
passed over and dried up all the
     waters

Charred Amazon palmtrees for
     hundreds of miles on both sides
     of the river

August 10, 1978

V—Waiting Room at the Rocky Flats Plutonium Plant

"Give us the weapons we need to protect ourselves!"
    the bareheaded guard lifts his flyswatter above the desk
                      —whap!

*

A green-letter'd shield on the pressboard wall!
    "Life is fragile. Handle with care"—
My Goodness! here's where they make the nuclear bomb-
        triggers.

August 17, 1978

VI — Numbers in Red Notebook

2,000,000 killed in Vietnam
13,000,000 refugees in Indochina 1972
200,000,000 years for the Galaxy to revolve on its core
24,000 the Babylonian Great Year
24,000 half life of plutonium
2,000 the most I ever got for a poetry reading
80,000 dolphins killed in the dragnet
4,000,000,000 years earth been born

Summer 1978

OLD POND

WORDS & TUNE: A. GINSBERG

AFTER BASHO

Th' OLD POND--a frog jumps in KER-PLUNK! HARD ROAD! I walked till both feet stunk-- MA! MA! Whatcha doin' down on that BED? PA! PA! what hole you hide your HEAD? LEFT home got work downtown to-DAY SOLD Coke, got busted looking GAY DAY dream, I acted like a CLUNK Th' OLD POND--a FROG JUMPS IN, KER-PLUNK!

DAVID MANSFIELD HELPED FIGURE OUT CHORDS IN BUFFALO, N.Y. 1978 · NOTATION BY STEVEN TAYLOR · MUSIC SCRIPT BY JON SHOLLE 1981

OLD POND

The old pond—a frog jumps in, kerplunk!
Hard road! I walked till both feet stunk—
Ma!Ma! Whatcha doing down on that bed?
Pa!Pa! what hole you hide your head?

        C
Left home   got work down town today
C   G
Sold coke,   got busted looking gay
G   C   F
Day dream, I acted like a clunk
F   C   F   G   C
Th'old pond—a frog jumps in, kerplunk!

Got hitched, I bought a frying pan
Fried eggs, my wife eats like a man
Won't cook, her oatmeal tastes like funk
Th'old pond—a frog jumps in, kerplunk!

Eat shit   exactly what she said
Drink wine, it goes right down my head
Fucked up, they all yelled I was drunk
Th'old pond—a frog jumps in, kerplunk!

Saw God at six o'clock tonight
Flop house, I think I'll start a fight
Head ache like both my eyeballs shrunk
Th'old pond—a frog jumps in, kerplunk!

Hot dog! I love my mustard hot
Hey Rube! I think I just got shot
Drop dead   She said you want some junk?
Th'old pond—a frog jumps in, kerplunk!

Oh ho   your dirty needle stinks
No no I don't shoot up with finks
Speed greed I stood there with the punk
Th'old pond—a frog jumps in, kerplunk!

Yeh yeh   gimme a breath of fresh air
Guess who   I am well you don't care
No name   call up the mocking Monk
Th'old pond—a frog jumps in, kerplunk!

No echo, make a lot of noise
Come home   you owe it to the boys
Can't hear   you scream your fish's sunk
Th'old pond—a frog jumps in, kerplunk!

Just folks, we bought a motor car
No gas   I guess we crossed the bar
I swear we started for Podunk
Th'old pond, a frog jumps in, kerplunk!

I got his banjo on my knee
I played it like an old Sweetie
I sang plunk-a-plunk-a-plunk plunk plunk plunk
Th'old pond—a frog jumps in, kerplunk!

One hand   I gave myself the clap
Unborn, but still I took the rap
Big deal, I fell out of my bunk
Th'old pond—a frog jumps in, kerplunk!

Hey hey! I ride down the blue sky
Sit down with worms until I die
Fare well! Hūṃ Hūṃ Hūṃ Hūṃ Hūṃ Hūṃ!
Th'old pond—a frog jumps in, kerplunk!

Red barn   rise wet in morning dew
Cockadoo   dle do oink oink moo moo
Buzz buzz—flyswatter in the kitchen, thwunk!
Th'old pond—a frog jumps in, kerplunk!

August 22, 1978

BLAME THE THOUGHT,
CLING TO THE BUMMER

I am Fake Saint
magazine Saint Ram Das
Who's not a Fake Saint consciousness, Nobody!
The 12th Trungpa, Karmapa 16, Dudjom lineage of Padma-
    sambhava, Pope Jean-Paul, Queen of England crowned
    with dignity's brilliant empty Diamonds Sapphires
    Emeralds, Amber, Rubies —
The sky is Fake Saint, emptyhearted blue
The Sacramento Valley floor fields no saints either, tractors
    in green corn higher than the T-shirted jogger.
This Volkswagen Fake Saint, license-plate-light wires smoking
    shorted in the rear-engine door.
Filter cigarette butt still smoking in the ashtray
No saints longhaired boys at the busdriver's wheel
Hard workers no Fake Saints laborers everywhere behind
    desks in Plutonium offices
swatting flies under plastic flower-power signs

Driving Ponderosa & Spruce roads to the poet's shrine at
    Kitkitdizze
Bedrock Mortar hermitage — Shobo-An temple's copper roof
    on a black-oak groved hillside —
Discontinuous, the thought — empty — no harm —
To blame the thought would cling to the Bummer —

Unborn Evil, the Self & its systems

Transitory intermittent gapped in Grass Valley stopping
    for gas

Plutonium blameless, apocalyptic Lamb of God

Insentient space filled with green bushes — clouds over Ranger
    Station signs

Uncertain as incense.

September 7, 1978

"DON'T GROW OLD"

I

Twenty-eight years before on the living room couch he'd
    stared at me, I said
"I want to see a psychiatrist — I have sexual difficulties —
    homosexuality"
I'd come home from troubled years as a student. This was the
    weekend I would talk with him.
A look startled his face, "You mean you like to take men's
    penises in your mouth?"
Equally startled, "No, no," I lied, "that isn't what it means."

Now he lay naked in the bath, hot water draining beneath
    his shanks.
Strong shouldered Peter, once ambulance attendant, raised
    him up
in the tiled room. We toweled him dry, arms under his,
    bathrobe over his shoulder —
he tottered thru the door to his carpeted bedroom
sat on the soft mattress edge, exhausted, and coughed up
    watery phlegm.
We lifted his swollen feet talcum'd white, put them thru
    pyjama legs,
tied the cord round his waist, and held the nightshirt sleeve
    open for his hand, slow.

Mouth drawn in, his false teeth in a dish, he turned his head
    round
rueful, looking up at Peter to smile, "Don't ever grow old."

II

At my urging, my eldest nephew came
to keep his grandfather company, maybe sleep overnight in
    the apartment.
He had no job, and was homeless anyway.
All afternoon he read the papers and looked at old movies.
Later dusk, television silent, we sat on a soft-pillowed couch,
Louis sat in his easy-chair that swivelled and could lean back —
"So what kind of job are you looking for?"
"Dishwashing, but someone told me it makes your hands'
    skin scaly red."
"And what about officeboy?" His grandson finished high-
    school with marks too poor for college.
"It's unhealthy inside airconditioned buildings under fluor-
    escent light."
The dying man looked at him, nodding at the specimen.
He began his advice. "You might be a taxidriver, but what if
    a car crashed into you? They say you can get mugged
    too.
"Or you could get a job as a sailor, but the ship could sink,
    you could get drowned.
"Maybe you should try a career in the grocery business, but

a box of bananas could slip from the shelf,
"you could hurt your head. Or if you were a waiter, you
could slip and fall down with a loaded tray, & have to
pay for the broken glasses.
"Maybe you should be a carpenter, but your thumb might
get hit by a hammer.
"Or a lifeguard—but the undertow at Belmar beach is dan-
gerous, and you could catch a cold.
"Or a doctor, but sometimes you could cut your hand with a
scalpel that had germs, you could get sick & die."

Later, in bed after twilight, glasses off, he said to his wife
"Why doesn't he comb his hair? It falls all over his eyes, how
can he see?
Tell him to go home soon, I'm too tired."

October 5, 1978

III

Resigned

A year before visiting a handsome poet and my Tibetan
guru,
Guests after supper on the mountainside
we admired the lights of Boulder spread glittering below
through a giant glass window—

After coffee, my father bantered wearily
"Is life worth living?   Depends on the liver—"
The Lama smiled to his secretary—
It was an old pun I'd heard in childhood.
Then he fell silent, looking at the floor
      and sighed, head bent heavy
          talking to no one—
              "What can you do . . .?"

October 6, 1978 *

See poems on death of Louis Ginsberg, Mind Breaths, *S.F.: City Lights, 1977, pps. 79-87*

LOVE RETURNED

Love returned with smiles
three thousand miles
to keep a year's promise
Anonymous, honest
studious, beauteous
learned and childlike
earnest and mild like
a student of truth,
a serious youth.

Whatever our ends
young and old we were friends
on the coast a few weeks
In New York now he seeks
scholarly manuscripts
old writs, haunted notes
Antique anecdotes,
rare libraries lain
back of the brain.

Now we are in bed
he kisses my head
his hand on my arm
holds my side warm
He presses my leg

I don't have to beg
his sweet penis heat
enlarged at my hip,
kiss his neck with my lip.

Small as a kid
his ass is not hid
I can touch, I can play
with his thighs any way
My cheek to his chest
my body's his guest
he offers his breast
his belly, the rest
hug and kiss to my bliss

Come twice at last
he offers his ass
first time for him
to be entered at whim
of my bare used cock —
his cheeks do unlock
tongue & hand at soft gland
Alas for my dreams
my part's feeble it seems

Familiar with lust
heartening the dust
of 50 years' boys'

abandoned love joys
Not to queer my idea
he's willing & trembles
& his body's nimble
where I want my hard skin
I can't get it on in.

Well another day comes
Church bells have rung
dawn blue in New York
I eat vegetables raw
Sun flowers, cole slaw
Age shortens my years
yet brings these good cheers
Some nights're left free
& Love's patient with me

December 16, 1978
6 am

DECEMBER 31, 1978

Shining Diamonds & Sequins glitter
    Grand Ballroom Waldorf
    Astoria on the TV Screen
radiant shifting goodbye to
    Times Square Phantoms
    waving
massed eyeglasses & umbrellas'
    rainy hands over
    heads
Celebrating China
    diplomatic relations
    Disco in Peking
Congressional black & tan faces
    on the news-dots sober Committee Report
    Concludes Conspiracy Killing
    Kennedy & Martin Luther King
President & Peacemaker last
    Decade departed
mysteriously gloomy miasma
    mind of NY Times Vietnam
    nuclear Warren Commission
    exploded, lies & confusion
popping firecrackers Razz-ma-Tazz
    in mylar hats under kleig lights
    dancing to Guy Lombardo

Hitchy Kitchy Koo in eyeglasses
      & bowties
with tinkling Pianos, Trombones
      & tubas above the round white
      champagne tables
Old Folks smiling into camera one
      last time
appreciating Royal Canadian
      Nostalgia
among sweepstake kitchen
      sinks & refrigerators
advertised before the deodorized
      stickup by Count Dracula
      with popping eyeballs.
How enthusiastic the soap ads
      while masses honk paper
      horns
between December's canyon'd building
walls straight-sided up
      thru red misted sky
      above Gotham
Broadway Omp-pa-pa-ing its
      regards to Heaven the
      umpteenth time,
tin Trumpets waiting to
      announce the year's
      midnight,
Big teeth having a good time,

        Puerto Ricans smiling
under 44th Street marquees
        greeting the camera's
        million-eyed blank
        Hope the itching's gone—
Live from New York! thousands
        scream delight
roaring the clock along simultaneous
        congratulations Network Chairman
        Wm. S. Paley—
Forgiveness! Time! the ball's
        falling down, drums
        roll loud
across America's speaker
        systems to
Balloons! Happy New Year!
        Trumpets & Bubbles wave
        thru the brain!
Raise yr hat & shake yr bracelet
        Telephone Edie! Blow yr Trumpet
        Ganymede with a mustache
Ring yr brazen horns ye
        Fire engines of Soho!
Bark ye dogges in lofts, explode
        yr honking halos ye
        weightless Angels of
        Television!

It's gonna be a delightful
     time, thank god nothing's
     happening muchachos
Tonite but parties & car crashes,
     births & ambulance sirens,
Confetti falling over
     heartbroken partygoers
     doing the Lindy Hop at the
     back window of the loft
years ago when Abstract-Expressionist
     painters & poets had a party
     celebrating U.S. Eternity
     on New Year's Eve before the War.

BROOKLYN COLLEGE BRAIN

for David Shapiro & John Ashbery

You used to wear dungarees & blue workshirt,
sneakers or cloth-top shoes, & ride alone
on subways, young & elegant unofficial
bastard of nature, sneaking sweetness into Brooklyn.
Now tweed jacket & yr father's tie on yr breast,
salmon-pink cotton shirt & Swedish bookbag
you're half bald, palsied lip & lower eyelid
continually tearing, gone back to college.
Goodbye Professor Ginsberg, get your identity
card next week from the front office so you can
get to class without being humiliated dumped on the
sidewalk by the black guard at the Student Union door.

Hello Professor Ginsberg have some coffee,
have some students, have some office hours
Tuesdays & Thursdays, have a couple subway tokens
in advance, have a box in the English Department,
have a look at Miss Sylvia Blitzer behind the typewriter
Have some poems er maybe they're not so bad have a
good time workshopping Bodhicitta in the Bird Room.

March 27, 1979

GARDEN STATE

It used to be, farms,
stone houses on green lawns
a wooded hill to play Jungle Camp
asphalt roads thru Lincoln Park.

The communists picnicked
amid spring's yellow forsythia
magnolia trees & apple blossoms, pale buds
breezy May, blue June.

Then came the mafia, alcohol
highways, garbage dumped in marshes, real
estate, World War II, money
flowed thru Nutley, bulldozers.

Einstein invented atom bombs
in Princeton, television antennae
sprung over West Orange—lobotomies
performed in Greystone State Hospital.

Old graveyards behind churches
on grassy knolls, Erie Railroad
bridges' Checkerboard underpass
signs, paint fading, remain.

Reminds me of a time pond's pure
water was green, drink or swim.
Taprock quarries embedded
with amethyst, quiet on Sunday.

I was afraid to talk to anyone
in Paterson, lest my sensitivity
to sex, music, the universe, be discovered &
I be laughed at, hit by colored boys.

"Mr. Professor" said the Dutchman
on Haledon Ave. "Stinky Jew" said
my friend black Joe, kinky haired.
Oldsmobiles past by in front of my eyeglasses.

Greenhouses stood by the Passaic in the sun,
little cottages in Belmar by the sea.
I heard Hitler's voice on the radio.
I used to live on that hill up there.

They threw eggs at Norman Thomas the Socialist speaker
in Newark Military Park, the police
stood by & laughed. Used to murder
silk strikers on Mill St. in the Twenties.

Now turn on your boob tube
They explain away the Harrisburg
hydrogen bubble, the Vietnam war,
They haven't reported the end of Jersey's gardens,

much less the end of the world.
Here in Boonton they made cannonballs
for Washington, had old iron mines,
spillways, coach houses — Trolleycars

ran thru Newark, gardeners dug up front lawns.
Look for the News in your own backyard
over the whitewashed picket fence, fading signs
on upper stories of red brick factories.

The Data Terminal people stand on Route 40
now. Let's get our stuff together. Let's
go back Sundays & sing old springtime music
on Greystone State Mental Hospital lawn.

Spring 1979

SPRING FASHIONS

Full moon over the shopping mall —
    in a display window's silent light
the naked mannequin observes her fingernails

Boulder 1979

LAS VEGAS: VERSES IMPROVISED FOR EL DORADO H.S. NEWSPAPER

Aztec sandstone waterholes known by Moapa've
dried out under the baccarat pits
of M.G.M.'s Grand Hotel.

If Robert Maheu knew
             who killed Kennedy
would he tell Santos Trafficante?

If Frank Sinatra had to grow his own
             food, would he learn
how to grind piñon nuts?

If Sammy Davis had to find original water
would he lead a million old ladies laughing
        round Mt. Charleston to the Sheepshead Mountains
                in migratory cycle?

Does Englebert know the name of
the mountains he sings in?

When gas and water dry up
will wild mustangs
        inhabit the Hilton Arcade?

Will the 130-billion-dollared-Pentagon guard
      the radioactive waste dump at Beatty
            for the whole Platonic Year?

Tell all the generals and Maitre D's
to read the bronze inscriptions
         under the astronomical flagpole at Hoover Dam.

Will Franklin Delano Roosevelt
         Bugsy Siegel and Buddha
all lose their shirts at Las Vegas?

Yeah! because they don't know how to gamble
      like mustangs and desert lizards.

September 23, 1979

TO THE PUNKS OF DAWLISH

Your electric hair's beautiful gold as Blake's Glad Day boy,
you raise your arms for industrial crucifixion
You get 45 Pounds a week on the Production line
and 15 goes to taxes, Mrs. Thatcher's nuclear womb swells
The Iron Lady devours your powers & hours your pounds
      and pride &
scatters radioactive urine on your mushroom dotted sheep
      fields.
"Against the Bourgeois!" you raise your lip & dandy costume
Against the Money Establishment you Pogo to garage bands
After humorous slavery in th' electronic factory
put silver pins in your nose, gold rings in your ears
talk to the Professor on the Plymouth train, asking
"Marijuana rots your brain like it says in the papers, insists
      on the telly?"
Cursed tragic kids rocking in a rail car on the Cornwall
      Coastline, Luck to your dancing revolution!
With bodies beautiful as the gold blond lads' of Oxford—
Your rage is more elegant than most purse-lipped considera-
      tions of Cambridge,
your mouths more full of slang & kisses than tea-sipping wits
      of Eton whispering over scones & clotted cream
conspiring to govern your music tax your body labor &
      chasten your impudent speech with an Official Secrets
      Act.

November 18, 1979

SOME LOVE

After 53 years
I still cry tears
I still fall in love
I still improve

My art with a kiss
My heart with bliss
My hands massage
Kids from the garage

Kids from the grave
Kids who slave
At study or labor
Still show me favor

How can I complain
When love like rain
Falls all over the land
On my head on my hand

On my breast on my shoes
Kisses arrive like foreign news
Mouths suck my cock
Boys wish me good luck

How long can I last
Such love gone past
So much to come
Till I get dumb

Rarer and rarer
Boys give me favor
Older and older
Love gets bolder

Sweeter and sweeter
Wrinkled like water
My skin still trembles
My fingers nimble

December 12, 1979

MAYBE LOVE

Maybe love will come
cause I am not so dumb
Tonight it fills my heart
heavy sad apart
from one or two I fancy
now I'm an old fairy.

This is hard to say
I've come to be this way
thru many loves of youth
that taught me most heart truth
Now I come by myself
in my hand a potbellied elf

It's not the most romantic
dream to be so frantic
for young men's bodies,
a fine sugar daddy
blest respected known
but left to bed alone.

How come love came to end
flaccid, how pretend
desires I have used
Four decades as I cruised
from bed to bar to book
Shamefaced like a crook

Stealing here & there
pricks & buttocks bare
by accident, by circumstance
Naivete or horny chance
stray truth or famous lie,
How come I came to die?

Love dies, body dies, the mind
keeps groping blind
half hearted full of lust
to wet the silken dust
of men that hold me dear
but won't sleep with me near.

This morning's cigarette
This morning's sweet regret
habit of many years
wake me to old fears
Under the living sun
one day there'll be no one

to kiss & to adore
& to embrace & more
lie down with side by side
tender as a bride
gentle under my touch —
Prick I love to suck.

Church bells ring again
in Heidelberg as when
in New York City town
I lay my belly down
against a boy friend's buttock
and couldn't get it up.

'Spite age and common Fate
I'd hoped love'd hang out late
I'd never lack for thighs
on which to sigh my sighs
This day it seems the truth
I can't depend on youth,

I can't keep dreaming love
I can't pray heav'n above
or call the pow'rs of hell
to keep my body well
occupied with young devils
tongueing at my navel.

I stole up from my bed
to that of a well-bred
young friend who shared my purse
and noted my tender verse,
I held him by the ass
waiting for sweat to pass

until he said Go back
I said that I would jack
myself away, not stay
& so he let me play
Allergic to my come —
I came, & then went home.

This can't go on forever,
this poem, nor my fever
for brown eyed mortal joy,
I love a straight white boy.
Ah the circle closes
Same old withered roses!

I haven't found an end
I can fuck & defend
& no more can depend
on youth time to amend
what old ages portend —
Love's death, & body's end.

Heidelberg 8 am Dec. 15 1979

RUHR-GEBIET

Too much industry
too much eats
too much beer
too much cigarettes

Too much philosophy
too many thought forms
not enough rooms—
not enough trees

Too much Police
too much computers
too much hi fi
too much Pork

Too much coffee
too much smoking
under grey slate roofs
Too much obedience

Too many bellies
Too many business suits
Too much paperwork
too many magazines

Too much industry
No fish in the Rhine
Lorelei poisoned
Too much embarrassment

Too many fatigued
workers on the train
Ghost Jews scream
on the streetcorner

Too much old murder
too much white torture
Too much one Stammheim
too many happy Nazis

Too many crazy students
Not enough farms
not enough Appletrees
Not enough nut trees

Too much money
Too many poor
turks without vote
"Guests" do the work

Too much metal
Too much fat
Too many jokes
not enough meditation

Too much anger
Too much sugar
Too many smokestacks
Not enough snow

Too many radioactive
plutonium wastebarrels
Take the Rhine gold
Build a big tomb

A gold walled grave
to bury this deadly nuclear slag
all the Banks' gold
Shining impenetrable

All the German gold
will save the Nation
Build a gold house
to bury the Devil

December 15, 1979

TUBINGEN-HAMBURG SCHLAFWAGEN

I

Why am I so angry at Kissinger?
      Kent State? Terrorism began in 1968!
"Berlin Student Protesting Shah Shot by Police."

II

Building lights above black water!
      passing over a big river, railroad bridge & tower.
Mmm Fairyland! Must be Frankfurt!

December 1979

WORDS & TUNE BY A.G.

LOVE FORGIVEN

TIME: AFTER CAMPION

STRAIGT & SLENDER YOUTHFUL TENDER LOVE SHOWS THE WAY AND NEVER SAYS NAY LIGHT & GENTLE-HEARTED MENTAL TONES SING & PLAY GUI-TAR IN BRIGHT-DAY VOICING ALWAYS MELODIES, PLEASE SING SAD, & SAY WHAT-EVER YOU MAY RIGHTEOUS HONEST HEARTS FORGIVENESS DRIVES WOES A-WAY, GIVES LOVE TO COLD CLAY

1979

NOTATION BY S. TAYLOR   MUSIC SCRIPT BY J. SHOLLE   1981

LOVE FORGIVEN

Straight and slender
Youthful tender
Love shows the way
And never says nay

Light & gentle-
Hearted mental
Tones sing & play
Guitar in bright day

Voicing always
Melodies, please
Sing sad, & say
Whatever you may

Righteous honest
Heart's forgiveness
Drives woes away,
Gives Love to cold clay

December 16, 1979

VERSES WRITTEN FOR STUDENT ANTIDRAFT REGISTRATION RALLY 1980

The Warrior is afraid
the warrior has a big trembling heart
the warrior sees bright explosions over Utah, a giant bomber
    moves over the hollow Mountain at Colorado Springs
the warrior laughs at its shadow, and flows out with his
    breath thru afternoon light
The warrior never goes to War
War runs away from the warrior's mouth
War falls apart in the warrior's mind
The Conquered go to War, drafted into shadow armies,
    navy'd on shadow oceans, flying in shadow fire
only helpless Draftees fight afraid, big meaty negroes trying
    not to die—
The Warrior knows his own sad & tender heart, which is not
    the heart of most newspapers
Which is not the heart of most Television—This kind of
    sadness doesn't sell popcorn
This kind of sadness never goes to war, never spends $100
    Billion on M.X. Missile systems, never fights shadows
    in Utah,
never hides inside a hollow mountain near Colorado Springs
    with Strategic Air Command
waiting orders that he press the Secret button to blow up all
    the Cities of Earth

March 15, 1980
Shambhala, Colorado

HOMEWORK

Homage Kenneth Koch

If I were doing my Laundry I'd wash my dirty Iran

I'd throw in my United States, and pour on the Ivory Soap,
scrub up Africa, put all the birds and elephants back in
the jungle,

I'd wash the Amazon river and clean the oily Carib & Gulf of
Mexico,

Rub that smog off the North Pole, wipe up all the pipelines
in Alaska,

Rub a dub dub for Rocky Flats and Los Alamos, Flush that
sparkly Cesium out of Love Canal

Rinse down the Acid Rain over the Parthenon & Sphinx,
Drain the Sludge out of the Mediterranean basin &
make it azure again,

Put some blueing back into the sky over the Rhine, bleach
the little Clouds so snow return white as snow,

Cleanse the Hudson Thames & Neckar, Drain the Suds out
of Lake Erie

Then I'd throw big Asia in one giant Load & wash out the
blood & Agent Orange,

Dump the whole mess of Russia and China in the wringer,
squeeze out the tattletail Gray of U.S. Central American
police state,

& put the planet in the drier & let it sit 20 minutes or an Aeon
till it came out clean.

April 26, 1980

AFTER WHITMAN & REZNIKOFF

1

What Relief

If my pen hand were snapped by a Broadway truck
—What relief from writing letters to the *Nation*
disputing tyrants, war gossip, FBI—
My poems'll gather dust in Kansas libraries,
adolescent farmboys opening book covers with ruddy hands.

2

Lower East Side

That round faced woman, she owns the street with her three
    big dogs,
screeches at me, waddling with her bag across Avenue B
Grabbing my crotch, "Why don't you talk to me?"
baring her teeth in a smile, loud voice like a taxi horn,
"Big Jerk . . . you think you're famous?"—reminds me of
    my mother.

3

I was in College Age Nineteen

My favorite Aunt Elanor always had a rheumatic heart,
            I hadn't seen her three months
Now she lay in a hospital bed, thin blue face on a pillow
                tubes wrapped in cellophane coming out of her arm
"My nephew Allen . . . Am I going to die?"
            I stared at her, "I—I—I don't know!"

April 29, 1980

REFLECTIONS AT LAKE LOUISE

I

At midnight the teacher lectures on his throne
Gongs, bells, wooden fish, tingling brass
Transcendent Doctrines, non-meditation, old dog barks
Past present future burn in Candleflame
incense fills intellects—
Mornings I wake, forgetting my dreams,
dreary hearted, lift my body out of bed
shave, wash, sit, bow down to the ground for hours.

II

Which country is real, mine or the teacher's?
Going back & forth I cross the Canada border, unguarded,
    guilty, smuggling 10,000 thoughts.

III

Sometimes my guru seems a Hell King, sometimes a King in
    Eternity,
    sometimes a newspaper story, sometimes familiar eyed
    father, lonely mother, hard working—

Poor man! to give me birth who may never grow up
    and earn my own living.

May 7, 1980

IV

Now the sky's clearer, clouds lifted, a patch of blue
shows above Mt. Victoria. I should go walking to the Plain of
    the Six Glaciers
but I have to eat Oryoki style, prostrate hours in the basement,
    study for Vajrayana Exams—
If I had a heart attack on the path around the lake would I be
    ready to face my mother?

Noon

V

Scandal in the Buddhafields
    The lake's covered with soft ice inches thick.
Naked, he insulted me under the glacier!
    He raped my mind on the wet granite cliffs!
He misquoted me in the white mists all over the *Nation*.
Hurrah! the Clouds drift apart!
    Big chunks of blue sky fall down!
Mount Victoria stands with a mouth full of snow.

VI

I wander this path along little Lake Louise, the teacher's too
busy to see me,
my dharma friends think I'm crazy, or worse, a lonely neurotic,
maybe I am —
Alone in the mountains, like in snowy streets of New York.

VII

Trapped in the Guru's Chateau surrounded by 300 disciples
I could go home to Cherry Valley, Manhattan, Nevada City
to be a farmer forever, die in Lower East Side slums, sit with
no lightbulbs in the forest,
Return to my daily mail Secretary, *Hard Times*, Junk mail
and love letters, get wrinkled old in Manhattan
Fly out and sing poetry, bring home windmills, grow tomatoes
and Marijuana
chop wood, do Zazen, obey my friends, muse in Gary's
Maidu Territory, study acorn mush,
Here I'm destined to study the Higher Tantras and be a
slave of Enlightenment.
Where can I go, how choose? Either way my life stands
before me,
mountains rising over the white lake 6 am, mist drifting
between water and sky.

May 7-9, 1980

"Τεθνάκην δ' ὀλίγω 'πιδεύησ φαίνομαι"

Red cheeked boyfriends tenderly kiss me sweet mouthed
under Boulder coverlets winter springtime
hug me naked laughing & telling girl friends
                    gossip till autumn

Ageing love escapes with his Childish body
Monday one man visited sleeping big cocked
older mustached crooked-mouthed not the same teen-
                    ager I sucked off

This kid comes on Thursdays with happy hard ons
long nights talking heart to heart reading verses
fucking hours he comes in me happy but I
                    can't get it in him

Cherub, thin-legged Southern boy once slept over
singing blues and drinking till he got horny
Wednesday night he gave me his ass I screwed him
                    good luck he was drunk

Blond curl'd clear eyed gardener passing thru town
teaching digging earth in the ancient One Straw
method lay back stomach bare that night blew me
                    I blew him and came

Winter dance Naropa a barefoot wild kid
jumped up grabbed me laughed at me took my hand and
ran out saying   Meet you at midnight your house
                    Woke me up naked

Midnight crawled in bed with me breathed in my ear
kissed my eyelids   mouth on his cock it was soft
"Doesn't do nothing for me," turned on belly
                    Came in behind him

Future youth I never may touch any more
Hark these Sapphics lipped by my hollow spirit
everlasting tenderness breathed in these vowels
                    sighing for love still

Song your cadence formed while on May night's full moon
yellow onions tulips in fresh rain pale grass
iris pea pods radishes grew as this verse
                    blossomed in dawn light

Measure forever his face eighteen years' old
green eyes blond hair muscular gold soft skin whose
god like boy's voice mocked me once three decades past
                    Come here and screw me

Breast struck   scared to look in his eyes   blood pulsing
my ears   mouth dry   tongue never moved ribs shook a
trembling fire ran down from my heart to my thighs
                    Love-sick to this day

Heavy limbed I sat in a chair and watched him
sleep naked all night afraid to kiss his mouth
tender dying waited for sun rise years a-
            go in Manhattan

May 17-June 1, 1980

FOURTH FLOOR, DAWN,
UP ALL NIGHT WRITING LETTERS

Pigeons shake their wings on the copper church roof
out my window across the street, a bird perched on the cross
surveys the city's blue-grey clouds. Larry Rivers
'll come at 10 AM and take my picture. I'm taking
your picture, pigeons. I'm writing you down, Dawn.
I'm immortalizing your exhaust, Avenue A bus.
O Thought, now you'll have to think the same thing forever!

6:48 am June 7, 1980

ODE TO FAILURE

Many prophets have failed, their voices silent
ghost-shouts in basements nobody heard dusty laughter in
    family attics
nor glanced them on park benches weeping with relief under
    empty sky
Walt Whitman viva'd local losers—courage to Fat Ladies in
    the Freak Show! nervous prisoners whose mustached
    lips dripped sweat on chow lines—
Mayakovsky cried, Then die! my verse, die like the workers'
    rank & file fusilladed in Petersburg!
Prospero burned his Power books & plummeted his magic
    wand to the bottom of dragon seas
Alexander the Great failed to find more worlds to conquer!
O Failure I chant your terrifying name, accept me your
    54 year old Prophet
epicking Eternal Flop! I join your Pantheon of mortal bards,
    & hasten this ode with high blood pressure
rushing to the top of my skull as if I wouldn't last another
    minute, like the Dying Gaul! to
You, Lord of blind Monet, deaf Beethoven, armless Venus
    de Milo, headless Winged Victory!
I failed to sleep with every bearded rosy-cheeked boy I
    jacked off over
My tirades destroyed no Intellectual Unions of KGB & CIA
    in turtlenecks & underpants, their woolen suits & tweeds

I never dissolved Plutonium or dismantled the nuclear Bomb
    before my skull lost hair
I have not yet stopped the Armies of entire Mankind in
    their march toward World War III
I never got to Heaven, Nirvana, X, Whatchamacallit, I never
    left Earth,
I never learned to die.

March 7-October 10, 1980

BIRDBRAIN!

Birdbrain runs the World!

Birdbrain is the ultimate product of Capitalism

Birdbrain chief bureaucrat of Russia, yawning

Birdbrain ran FBI 30 years appointed by F. D. Roosevelt
and never chased the Mafia!

Birdbrain apportions wheat to be burned, keep prices up on
the world market!

Birdbrain lends money to Developing Nation police-states
thru the World Bank!

Birdbrain never gets laid on his own he depends on his
office to pimp for him

Birdbrain offers brain transplants in Switzerland

Birdbrain wakes up in middle of night and arranges his
sheets

I am Birdbrain!

I rule Russia Yugoslavia England Poland Argentina United
States El Salvador

Birdbrain multiplies in China!

Birdbrain inhabits Stalin's corpse in the Kremlin wall

Birdbrain dictates petrochemical agriculture in Afric desert
regions!

Birdbrain lowers North California's water table sucking it
up for Agribusiness Banks

Birdbrain harpoons whales and chews blubber in the tropics

Birdbrain clubs baby harp seals and wears their coats to
Paris

Birdbrain runs the Pentagon his brother runs the CIA, Fatass
 Bucks!

Birdbrain writes and edits *Time Newsweek Wall Street Journal*

Birdbrain is Pope, Premier, President, Commissar, Chairman,
 Senator!

Birdbrain voted Reagan President of the United States !

Birdbrain prepares Wonder Bread with refined white flour!

Birdbrain sold slaves, sugar, tobacco, alcohol

Birdbrain conquered the New World and murdered mushroom
 god Xochopili on Popocatepetl!

Birdbrain was President when a thousand mysterious stu-
 dents were machinegunned at Tlatelolco

Birdbrain sent 20,000,000 intellectuals and Jews to Siberia,
 15,000,000 never got back to the Stray Dog Café

Birdbrain wore a mustache & ran Germany on Amphetamines
 the last year of World War II

Birdbrain conceived the Final Solution to the Jewish Prob-
 lem in Europe

Birdbrain carried it out in Gas Chambers

Birdbrain borrowed Lucky Luciano from the Mafia to secure
 Sicily for Birdbrain against the Reds

Birdbrain manufactured guns in the Holy Land and sold
 them to white goys in South Africa and Birdbrain
 supplied helicopters to Central America tyrants so they
 killed a lot of restless Indians

Birdbrain began a war of terror against Israeli Jews

Birdbrain sent out Zionist planes to shoot Palestinian huts
 outside Beirut

Birdbrain outlawed Opiates on the world market

Birdbrain formed the Black Market in Opium

Birdbrain's father bought skag in lower East Side hallways

Birdbrain organized Operation Condor to spray poison fumes
    on the marijuana fields of Sonora

Birdbrain got sick in Harvard Square from smoking Mexi-
    can grass

Birdbrain arrived in Europe to Conquer cockroaches with
    Propaganda

Birdbrain became a great International Poet and went around
    the world praising the Glories of Birdbrain

Birdbrain isn't evil, he just don't talk good, he's Sympathetic—

I declare Birdbrain to be victor in the Poetry Contest

He built the World Trade Center on New York Harbor with-
    out regard where toilets emptied—

Birdbrain began chopping down the Amazon Rainforest to
    build a woodpulp factory on the river bank

Birdbrain in Iraq attacked Birdbrain in Iran

Birdbrain in Belfast throws bombs at his mother's ass

Birdbrain wrote *Das Kapital*

Birdbrain authored the *Bible*! penned a *Wealth of Nations*!

Birdbrain is humanity, he built the Rainbow Room on top of
    Rockefeller Center so we could dance

He invented the Theory of Relativity so Rockwell could
    make Neutron Bombs in Colorado

Birdbrain's going to see how long he can go without coming

Birdbrain thinks his dong will grow big that way

Birdbrain sees a new Spy in the Market Platz in Dubrovnik
    outside the Eyeglass Hotel—

Birdbrain wants to suck your cock in Europe, he takes life
    very seriously, brokenhearted you won't cooperate—
Birdbrain goes to heavy duty Communist Countries so he
    can get KGB girlfriends while the sky thunders—
Birdbrain became Buddha by meditating
Birdbrain's afraid he's going to blow up the planet so he
    built this Rocket to get away—

Hotel Subrovka, Dubrovnik,
October 14, 1980, 4:30 am

EROICA

White marble pillars in the Rector's courtyard
at the end of a marble-white street in the walled city of
  Dubrovnik—
All the fleet sunk, Empire foundered, Doges all skeletons
  & Turks vanished to dust
World Wars passed by with cannonfire mustard gas & ampheta-
  mine-wired Führers—
Beethoven's drum roll beats again in the stone household
White jackets and Black ties the makers of Dissonant thun-
  derbolts concentrate on music sheets
Bowing low, the Timpanist bends ear to his Copper Kettle-
  drums' heroic vibration—
Bassists with hornrim glasses and beards, young and old
  pluck ensemble with middle fingers at thin animal
  strings—
Bassoonists press lips to wooden hollow wands,
The Violinists fiddle up and down excitedly—First Violin
with a stubborn beard (at his music stand with a young
  girl in black evening dress) waits patiently the orchestra
  tuning and tweedling to a C—
The Conductor moves his baton & elbows to get the Beethoven
  bounce jumping
Sweating in the cool Adriatic air at 10:15 white collar round
  his neck, black longtailed jacket & celluloid cuffs, high
  heeled black shoes—he turns the glossy page of the
  First Movement—

The brasses ring out, trumpets puffing, French horns blaring
    for Napoleon!
Conductor whips it to a Bam Bam Bamb.

But Beethoven got disgusted with Napoleon & scratched his
    hero name off the Dedication page—

Now the Funeral March! I used to listen to this over the
    radio in Paterson during the Spanish Civil War—
At last I know it's the bassoons Carry the wails of high elegy
at last I see the cellos in their chairs, violinists swaying
    forward, bassmen standing looking sad
as all bow together the mournful lament & dead march for
    Europe,
The end of the liberty of Dubrovnik, the idiot cry March
    on Moscow!
Dubrovnik's musicians take revenge on Napoleon,
by playing Beethoven's heroic chords in a Castle by the
    sea at Night—
Electric Globes on wrought iron stands light the year 1980
    (Emperor Napoleon & Emperor Beethoven alike snoring
    skulls)
in the Rector's house reconstructed a Concert Hall for
    Tourists
Beethoven's heart pulses in the drums, his breath¹ uffs and
    puffs, the violin arms of the black robed lady & the
    bearded Concert-master swing

The Funeral Fugue Begins! The Death of Kings, the scream-
ing of Revolutionary multitudes
as the Middle Ages tumble before the Industrial Revolution
a Mysterious Clarion! an extended brassy breath!
serene rows of island cities in violin language,
working back and forth from violins to bassoons—
The drum beats the footfalls of Coffin Carriers—
over the roofs the lilt of a sad melody emerges,
like silent cats on red tile, the strings Climb up sadder—
a broken-muzzled lion's head sticks out of a white plaster
Fountain wall in the courtyard
Now rats and lions chase each other round the orchestra
from fiddle string to bass gut staccato—
Hunting horns echo mellow against marble staircase blocks—
Napoleon has himself crowned Emperor by the Pope!
Unbelievable! Atom Bombs drop on Japan! Hitler attacks
Poland! The Allies fire-bomb Dresden alive! America
goes to war—
Now Violins and Horns rise Counterpoint to a thunderous
bombing! Kettledrums war up! Bam Bamb! End of
Scherzo!

Finale—Tiptoeing thru history, Pizzicato on the Bass Cello
& Violins as Time marches on.
Running thru the veins, the lilt of victory, the Liberation of
man from the State!
It's a big dance, a festival, every instrument joined in the
Yea Saying!

Who wouldn't be happy meeting Beethoven at Jena in 1812
or 1980! It's a small world, standing up to sing like a big
beating heart!
Getting ready for the Ecstatic European Dance! Off we go on
one ear, then another, Titanic Footsteps over Middle
Europe—
And a waltz to quiet down the joy, But the big dance will
come back like Eternity like God like
a hurricane an Earthquake a Beethoven Creation
a new Europe! A new world of Liberty almost 200 years ago
Prophesied thru brass and catgut, wood bow & breath
Gigantic Heartbeat of Beethoven's Deaf Longing—
The Prophecy of a Solid happy peaceful Just Europe—
Big as the Trumpets of the Third Symphony.
The Unification of the World! The triumph of the Moon!
Mankind liberated to Music!
Enough to make you cry in the middle of the Rector's Palace,
thinking of Einstein's
Atom Bomb exploded out of his head—
In the middle of a note, an interruption! Cloudburst!
The Conductor wipes his head & runs away,
basses and cellos lift up their woods and vanish into Cloak-
rooms,
French Horns Violins and Bassoons lift eyes to the shower &
scatter under balconies
in the middle for a note, in the middle of a big Satyric
Footstep,

Pouf! Rain pours thru the sky!
Musicians and audience flee the stone floor'd courtyard,
Atrium of the Rectors House Dubrovnik October 14, 1980,
       10:45 p.m.

"DEFENDING THE FAITH"

Stopping on the bus from Novi Pazar in the rain
I took a leak by Maglic Castle walls
and talked with the dogs on Ivar River Bank
They showed me their teeth & barked a long time.

October 20, 1980

CAPITOL AIR

WORDS: A. GINSBERG

--ALSO MUSIC 1980-1

I DON'T LIKE THE GOVERNMENT WHERE I LIVE!

I DON'T LIKE DICTATOR - SHIP OF THE RICH!

I DON'T LIKE BUREAUCRATS TELLING ME WHAT TO EAT!

I DON'T LIKE POLICE DOGS SNIFFING A - ROUND MY FEET!

NOTATION BY STEVEN TAYLOR 1981   MUSIC SCRIPT BY JON SHOLLE 1981

"NO HOPE COMMUNISM NO HOPE CAPITALISM YEAH!
EVERYBODY'S LYING ON BOTH SIDES NYEAH NYEAH NYEAH!"

CAPITOL AIR

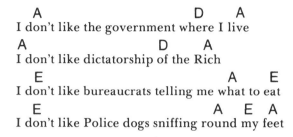

```
  A                    D      A
I don't like the government where I live
  A                    D      A
I don't like dictatorship of the Rich
    E                         A      E
I don't like bureaucrats telling me what to eat
    E                       A   E   A
I don't like Police dogs sniffing round my feet
```

I don't like Communist Censorship of my books
I don't like Marxists complaining about my looks
I don't like Castro insulting members of my sex
Leftists insisting we got the mystic Fix

I don't like Capitalists selling me gasoline Coke
Multinationals burning Amazon trees to smoke
Big Corporation takeover media mind
I don't like the Top-bananas that're robbing Guatemala
     banks blind

I don't like K.G.B. Gulag concentration camps
I don't like the Maoists' Cambodian Death Dance
15 Million were killed by Stalin Secretary of Terror
He has killed our old Red Revolution for ever

I don't like Anarchists screaming Love Is Free
I don't like the C.I.A. they killed John Kennedy
Paranoiac tanks sit in Prague and Hungary
But I don't like counterrevolution paid for by the C.I.A.

Tyranny in Turkey or Korea Nineteen Eighty
I don't like Right Wing Death Squad Democracy
Police State Iran Nicaragua yesterday
Laissez-faire please Government keep your secret police offa me

I don't like Nationalist Supremacy White or Black
I don't like Narcs & Mafia marketing Smack
The General bullying Congress in his tweed vest
The President building up his Armies East & West

I don't like Argentine police assassinating Jews
Government Terrorist takeover Salvador news
I don't like Zionists acting Nazi Storm Troop
Palestine Liberation cooking Israel into Moslem soup

I don't like the Crown's Official Secrets Act
You can get away with murder in the Government that's a fact
Security cops teargassing radical kids
In Switzerland or Czechoslovakia God Forbids

In America it's Attica in Russia it's Lubianka Wall
In China if you disappear you wouldn't know yourself at all
Arise Arise you citizens of the world use your lungs
Talk back to the Tyrants all they're afraid of is your tongues

Two hundred Billion dollars inflates World War
In United States every year They're asking for more
Russia's got as much in tanks and laser planes
Give or take Fifty Billion we can blow out everybody's brains

School's broke down 'cause History changes every night
Half the Free World nations are Dictatorships of the Right
The only place socialism works is in asterisks bud
The Communist world's stuck together with prisoner's blood

The Generals say they know something worth fighting for
They never say what till they start an unjust war
Iranian hostage Media Hysteria sucks
The Shah ran away with 9 Billion Iranian bucks

Col. Roosevelt and his U.S. dollars overthrew Mossadeq
They wanted his oil then they got Ayatollah's dreck
They put in the Shah and they trained his police the Savak
All Iran was our hostage quarter-century That's right Jack

Bishop Romero wrote President Carter to stop
Guns to El Salvador's Junta so he got shot
Ambassador White blew the whistle on the White House lies
Reagan called him home cause he looked in dead nuns' eyes

Half the voters didn't vote they knew it was too late
Newspaper headlines called it a big Mandate
Some people voted for Reagan eyes open wide
3 out of 4 didn't vote for him That's a Landslide

Truth may be hard to find but Falsehood's easy
Read between the lines our Imperialism is sleazy
If you think the People's State is your Heart's Desire
Jump right back in the frying pan from the fire

The System the System in Russia & China the same
Criticize the System in Budapest lose your name
Coca Cola Pepsi Cola in Russia & China come true
Khrushchev yelled in Hollywood "We will bury You"

America and Russia want to bomb themselves Okay
Everybody dead on both sides   Everybody pray
All except the Generals in caves where they can hide
And fuck each other in the ass waiting for the next free ride

No hope Communism no hope Capitalism Yeah
Everybody's lying on both sides Nyeah nyeah nyeah
The bloody iron curtain of American Military Power
Is a mirror image of Russia's red Babel-Tower

Jesus Christ was spotless but was Crucified by the Mob
Law & Order Herod's hired soldiers did the job
Flowerpower's fine but innocence has got no Protection
The man who shot John Lennon had a Hero-worshipper's
      connection

The moral of this song is that the world is in a horrible place
Scientific Industry devours the human race
Police in every country armed with Tear Gas & TV
Secret Masters everywhere bureaucratize for you & me

Terrorists and police together build an upperclass Rage
Propaganda murder manipulates the middleclass Stage
Can't tell the difference 'tween a turkey & a provocateur
If you're feeling confused the Government's in there for sure

Aware Aware wherever you are   No Fear
Trust your heart Don't ride your Paranoia dear
Breathe together with an ordinary mind
Armed with Humor Feed & Help Enlighten Woe Mankind

Frankfurt — New York
December 15, 1980

BY ALLEN GINSBERG

Poetry Books

Howl and Other Poems. City Lights Books, SF, 1956.
Kaddish and Other Poems. City Lights Books, SF, 1961.
Empty Mirror, Early Poems. Totem/Corinth, NY, 1961.
Reality Sandwiches. City Lights Books, SF, 1963.
Ankor Wat. Fulcrum Press, London, 1968 (O.P.)
Planet News. City Lights Books, SF, 1968.
The Gates of Wrath, Rhymed Poems 1948-51. Four Seasons, Bolinas, 1972.
The Fall of America, Poems of These States. City Lights Books, SF, 1973.
Iron Horse. Coach House Press, Toronto/City Lights Books, SF, 1973.
First Blues. Full Court Press, NY, 1975.
Mind Breaths, Poems 1971-76. City Lights Books, SF, 1978.
Poems All Over the Place, Mostly '70s. Cherry Valley Ed., Cherry Valley, NY, 1978.
Plutonian Ode, Poems 1977-1980. City Lights Books, SF, 1982.

Prose Books

The Yage Letters. (w/Wm S. Burroughs), City Lights Books, SF, 1963.
Indian Journals. David Hazelwood/City Lights Books, SF, 1970.

Gay Sunshine Interview. Grey Fox Press, Bolinas, 1974.

Allen Verbatim: Lectures on Poetry etc. McGraw Hill, NY, 1974.

Chicago Trial Testimony. City Lights Ashcan of History Series #1, SF, 1975.

To Eberhart from Ginsberg. Penmaen Press, Lincoln, Mass., 1976.

Journals Early Fifties Early Sixties. Grove Press, NY, 1977.

As Ever: Collected Correspondence Allen Ginsberg & Neal Cassady. Creative Arts, Berkeley, 1977.

Composed on the Tongue. Grey Fox Press, Bolinas, 1980.

Anthologies, Interviews, Essays, Bibliographies

The New American Poetry 1945-1960. (D. Allen, ed.), Grove Press, NY, 1960.

A Casebook of the Beat. (T. Parkinson, ed.), Thomas Y. Crowell, NY, 1961.

The Marihuana Papers. (D. Solomon, ed.), Bobbs-Merrill, NY, 1961.

Paris Review Interviews. (w/Tom Clark), 3rd Series, Viking, NY, 1967.

The Poem in Its Skin. (P. Carrol, ed.), Big Table/Follet, Chicago, 1968.

Playboy. (interview w/Paul Carrol), 1969.

Scenes Along the Road. (A. Charters, Ed.), Gotham Book Mart, NY, 1970.

Poetics of the New American Poetry. (D. Allen & W. Tallman, eds.), Grove, NY, 1973.

The Beat Books. (A. & G. Knight, eds.), California, Pa., 1974 et seq.

The New Naked Poetry. (Berg & Mexey, eds.), Bobbs-Merrill, NY, 1976.

Visionary Poetics of Allen Ginsberg. Paul Portuges, Ross-Erikson, Santa Barbara, 1978.

Talking Poetics From Naropa Institute. (Waldman & Webb, eds.), Shambhala, Boulder, Vol. 1: 1978, Vol. 2: 1979.

Allen Ginsberg Bibliography 1943-1967. (G. Dowden, ed.), City Lights Books, SF, 1971.

Allen Ginsberg Bibliography 1969-1978. (M. Kraus, ed.) Scarecrow Press, NJ, 1980.

Phonograph Records

Howl and Other Poems. Fantasy-Galaxy Records #7013, Berkeley, 1959.

Kaddish. Atlantic Verbum Series 4001, NY, 1966. (O.P.)

Wm Blake's Songs of Innocence & of Experience Tuned by A.G., MGM Records, NY, 1970 (O.P.)

Blake Album II. Fantasy-Galaxy Records, 1971. (unissued)

Gaté. Vol. 1, Songs. LOFT 1001Stereo, Munich, 1980. Dist. Germany, zweitausendeins; Dist. U.S., City Hall Records, SF.

First Blues, Harmonium Rags and Rock & Roll. Double album, John Hammond Records, NY, 1982.

POCKET POETS SERIES

1.: Lawrence Ferlinghetti. *Pictures of a Gone World*. $2.00
3: Kenneth Patchen. *Poems of Humor and Protest*. $1.50
4: Allen Ginsberg. *Howl and Other Poems*. $2.00
7: William Carlos Williams. *Kora in Hell*. $2.00
8: Gregory Corso. *Gasoline/Vestal Lady*. $2.95
9: Jacques Prevert. *Paroles*. $2.50
13: Kenneth Patchen. *Love Poems*. $2.00
14: Allen Ginsberg. *Kaddish and Other Poems*. $2.50
16: Yevgeny Yevtushenko, et al. *Red Cats*. $1.00
17: Malcolm Lowry. *Selected Poems*. $2.00
18: Allen Ginsberg. *Reality Sandwiches*. $2.50
19: Frank O'Hara. *Lunch Poems*. $2.50
20: Philip Lamantia. *Selected Poems*. $1.50
21: Bob Kaufman. *Golden Sardine*. $2.00
23: Allen Ginsberg. *Planet News*. $2.95
24: Charles Upton. *Panic Grass*. $1.00
27: Diane DiPrima. *Revolutionary Letters*. $3.50
28: Jack Kerouac. *Scattered Poems*. $2.00
29: Andrei Voznesensky. *Dogalypse*. $1.50
30: Allen Ginsberg. *The Fall of America*. $4.00
31: Pete Winslow. *A Daisy in the Memory of a Shark*. $2.00
33: Anne Waldman. *Fast Speaking Woman*. $3.00
34: Jack Hirschman. *Lyripol*. $2.50
35: Allen Ginsberg. *Mind Breaths*. $3.50
36: Stefan Brecht. *Poems*. $3.50
37: Peter Orlovsky. *Clean Asshole Poems & Smiling Vegetable Songs*. $3.95
38: Antler. *Factory*. $3.00
39: Philip Lamantia. *Becoming Visible*. $3.95
40: Allen Ginsberg. *Plutonian Ode and Other Poems*. $4.95